MW00963596

SOME ASSEMBLY REQUIRED

Eugene Stickland

Eugene Stickland (signature)

Andy –

It's always so comforting – especially
these previews – to see you in
the lobby and to know you are
here. Have a great Christmas and all
that. Love
Eugene

COTEAU BOOKS

Edited by Dave Margoshes.
Cover design by Dik Campbell.
Cover photograph by Zak Hauser. Author photo by Thom Laycraft.
Book design and typesetting by Val Jakubowski.
Printed and bound in Canada.

The author wishes to thank Bob White and Charlotte Lee for their encouragement and guidance, the Saskatchewan Arts Board for financial assistance and the Saskatchewan Playwrights Centre for a developmental workshop. Further thanks to Digital Equipment of Canada, Ltd., the Auburn Saloon, Louis Neuman and, as always, Carrie Schiffler.

The publisher gratefully acknowledges the financial assistance of the Saskatchewan Arts Board, the Canada Council, the Department of Canadian Heritage, and the City of Regina Arts Commission.

Excerpt from "Journey of the Magi" in COLLECTED POEMS 1909-1962 by T.S. Eliot, copyright 1936 by Harcourt Brace & Company, and by Faber and Faber Limited, copyright © 1964, 1963 by T.S. Eliot, reprinted by permission of the publishers.

Excerpt from "On the Street Where You Live," a song from *My Fair Lady* by Alan Jay Lerner and Frederick Loewe, © 1956 by Chappell & Co. All Rights Reserved. Used By Permission.

Canadian Cataloguing in Publication Data

Stickland, Eugene, 1956-

Some assembly required

(Florence James series ; 8)
A play.
ISBN 1-55050-090-2

I. Title. II. Series.

PS8587.T553S6 1995   C812'.54   C95-920135-1
PR9199.3.S853S6 1995

COTEAU BOOKS
401 - 2206 Dewdney Avenue
Regina, Saskatchewan
Canada S4R 1H3

For Tom

Anxiety. Guilt. Paranoia. Fear of failure. The inability to communicate. Is this the stuff of comedy? All good comedies are about very serious things, and *Some Assembly Required* is no exception. But it is a rarity among Canadian plays that have emerged in the mid-nineties. Much of our contemporary drama appears overly preoccupied with the individual's pursuit of identity in an incomprehensible world. And this search is often presented in a pretentious, self-conscious manner. *Some Assembly Required* is a bona fide comedy. Eugene Stickland has the insight to situate his version of the identity quest in a particularly rich source of comedic possibilities: the family. While family affairs have been the touchstone of drama from Aeschylus through Eugene O'Neill to Sam Shepard, it could be argued that, among our own playwrights, only George Walker has consistently mined the comic possibilities of the ties of blood. Eugene Stickland embraces the inevitable truth that we can't avoid the fact that we've been shaped by our families and those experiences may have an awful lot to do with why we are the way we are. Those vacations with everybody packed in an overheated car. The supper's going cold while we wait for Dad to come home. And then there's Christmas.

The popularity of *Some Assembly Required* has much to do with the familiarity of the dramatic premise of the play. A family reluctantly gathers together on Christmas Eve. In production, the play provokes intermission and postshow revelations of our own Christmas horror stories. It seems to come as a relief to everybody to acknowledge that life really has nothing to do with the world portrayed on the "Anne Murray Christmas Special." Curiously, though, despite this acknowledgment that the myths of Christmas and family bonding are just that – myths that speak to our fantasies – the play is far from cynical or bleak. It's as if by naming our fears, we can find a form of liberation and move on. There isn't a conventional happy ending to *Some Assembly Required*, but there is an odd, touching hope. The wonderfully sad, and hysterically funny, forced singing of "O Christmas Tree" at gunpoint says it all. We may be the dysfunctional family from hell, but can't we at least try?

And there is hope because we care about these characters. They are all wonderfully idiosyncratic and compelling. It is testament to the playwright's skill that we can identify with five characters so engrossed in their own failures they can barely register each other's presence. These are losers – big time. But we know they want better for themselves – and for those about them. Stacy's insistence on finding a way to "turn the page" reverberates across the stage and through the theatre. We want this family to have a "real" Christmas, because if they succeed maybe we can break out of our own failures and move on as well.

It is this "common touch" that makes Eugene Stickland an important writer. Although he writes many different kinds of plays, he has an uncanny ability to speak to the hopes and fears of ordinary people in ordinary situations. *Some Assembly Required* isn't critically fashionable writing. It doesn't attempt to redefine theatrical form. Or articulate the state of human consciousness on the brink of the millennium. Or, thank god, chart the bruisings the sensitive artist encounters in an unfeeling world. *Some Assembly Required* is about engaging an audience at a very basic level. Most of us have pretty simple aspirations. We want to be happy, and we want those around us to be happy, too. In addressing this kind of need, Eugene Stickland represents the kind of writing we want more of in this country. Plays about people, not ideology. Plays with heart. Plays that aren't scornful of the audience. And, perhaps most importantly, plays that are filled with the joys and disappointments of ordinary life.

Some Assembly Required has been labeled a "Christmas" play. I think it is a play for all seasons. Although the play spends a lot of time debunking the rituals of Christmas, it actually is about the real meaning of the Christmas story: redemption. And to pull that off in a play filled with wit and laughs by the punch bowlfull is no mean feat. *Some Assembly Required* should be seen anytime tidings of comfort and joy are called for, and I should think audiences are ready to welcome this celebration of real family values just about anytime of the year.

Bob White
Alberta Theatre Projects
Calgary, June, 1995

"A cold coming we had of it,
Just the worst time of the year
For a journey, and such a long journey:
The ways deep and the weather sharp,
The very dead of winter."

T.S. Eliot, *Journey of the Magi*

PREMIERE PRODUCTION

Some Assembly Required was first produced by Alberta Theatre Projects, D. Michael Dobbin, producing director, as part of *playRites '94*, sponsored in part by Shell Canada Ltd., with the following cast:

DAD . . . . Robert Benson
MOTHER . . . . Anne McGrath
WALTER . . . . Neil Barclay
GORDON . . . . Christopher Hunt
STACY . . . . Marianne Copithorne

DIRECTOR . . . . D.D. Kugler
SET DESIGNER . . . . John Dinning
COSTUME DESIGNER . . . . Carolyn Smith
LIGHTING DESIGNER . . . . Harry Frehner
PRODUCTION DRAMATURGE . . . . . . Bob White
PRODUCTION STAGE MANAGER . . . . Dianne Goodman
STAGE MANAGER . . . . Charlotte Green

CHARACTERS

MOTHER
DAD
WALTER
GORDON
STACY

SETTING

A comfortable house in the old part of town. The action takes place either in the basement, which has been transformed into GORDON's *living space, the living room/dining room or in* MOTHER's *bedroom.*

THE TIME

Christmas Eve.

ACT ONE

SCENE ONE

The stage is dark. A small but powerful flashlight clicks on. It is focused on the eye of a woman.

If the light were to spill over, we would see that it is DAD *who has crept into* MOTHER's *room. After a few moments,* MOTHER, *who is lying on her back on a gurney, reacts to* DAD's *ministrations, as the lights come up on the bedroom.*

DAD: Pupils contracting. Very good. Very normal. Eyes respond to light. Just as it should be. A normal response. This is a good sign, my dear (*Directs light toward his notebook*) ... just make a notation of this in the old notebook: "Eyes-colon-normal-response-period." Now. If we could just get the rest of you to follow the example of your eyes, I'm sure you'd be up and at 'em in no time.

MOTHER *sits up. Now both are visible in a faint, grey light.*

MOTHER: What on earth are you doing?

DAD: You're awake!

MOTHER: You're shining a flashlight in my eye.

DAD: I'm checking.

MOTHER: Checking?

DAD: That's correct.

MOTHER: Checking what?

DAD: I'm checking to see if your eyes respond to the light.

MOTHER: And?

DAD: Looks normal to me.

MOTHER: Get that thing away from me. And get me some water.

DAD: Sure thing.

MOTHER: My mouth is so dry.

DAD: Just as Doctor Bob predicted.

MOTHER: I didn't think one could be so dry, and still alive.

DAD: It's a perfectly normal reaction. Perfectly normal. Nothing to worry about. There you go. Better?

MOTHER: Dust. I'm made of dust.

DAD: Well … a little water, a little rest….

Pause.

MOTHER: Just the thought of Gordon, holed up down the basement! It's more than I can stand!

DAD: Yes, I know what you're saying. I have a dark fear that he has been tampering with my barbed wire, agitating my samples. I don't let myself think what he might be doing with my power tools! My router … my three speed cordless rechargeable reversible Makita hand drill!

MOTHER: Who cares about your old tools? I'm talking about Gordon. Our youngest child. My baby! My baby!

DAD: OK, Sweetheart. That's OK. I don't think we want to test these particular waters right now. Let's just try to keep on our course here, shall we?

MOTHER: But today of all days!

DAD: It's just another day, Charlotte. Just another day. With any luck, it'll soon be over and then we'll move on. Right?

MOTHER: I suppose….

DAD: OK.

MOTHER: But what if Gordon comes up?

DAD: Gordon's not coming up! How many times do I have to tell you? He's not coming up! OK?

She lies back down and turns her back to him.

DAD: OK?

No response.

DAD: Ah, for Pete's … I'm sorry. I'm sorry.

Pause.

DAD: I'll just be out there, listening to my records.

Lights fade to blackout. The flashlight comes back on and wobbles across the stage.

Scene Two

DAD *enters the living room. With great care and white cotton gloves, he puts an album on the turntable: Dean Martin singing "Everybody Loves Somebody Sometime." Lights come up on the living room.* DAD *sits down in the recliner, nursing a rye and water, writing in his notebook.*

The room seems comfortable and homey at first glance. On closer inspection, however, we notice that the couch, chair and lamp shades are protected with plastic. The fireplace is obviously artificial. Other than this, the room is remarkable for the plaque hanging above the fireplace on which short strands of several different types of barbed wire are displayed. Beside this hangs an old-fashioned portrait of Lucien Smith.

After a moment, WALTER *enters, unseen by* DAD. *He is carrying a suitcase and dressed for an Arctic expedition. He takes off his parka, galoshes and other survival gear, and is careful to hide his suitcase.*

WALTER: Hello, Dad!

DAD *doesn't hear.* WALTER *comes around.*

WALTER: Hello, Dad!

DAD: Walter!

WALTER: Merry Christmas!

DAD: What in the name of thunder are you doing back here?

WALTER: It's Christmas, Dad!

DAD: So?

WALTER: I thought I'd spend it here, back here, in the bosom of my family.

WALTER *warms his hands at the artificial fireplace.*

WALTER: Ahhhhh ... A little nippy out there. 37 below. Windchill factor of 2100. They say exposed human flesh can freeze in less than a minute.

He pulls and plucks at his face to see if he is frozen. As he is doing this, he notes that there are no Christmas decorations or such.

WALTER: No stockings this year, Dad? No yule log? No tree?!

DAD: After careful consideration, your mother and I decided that a tree, like many other aspects of the Christmas celebration, such as your stockings and yule logs, is grossly overrated.

WALTER: But Dad!

DAD: Besides, we weren't anticipating company.

WALTER: OK, Dad.

DAD: Why would we expect that anyone, least of all our children, would take time from their busy schedules and look in on us on Christmas Eve?

WALTER: I'm sorry, dad.

DAD: You're sorry.

WALTER: What can I say? I've had a tough go of it.

DAD: I'm sure. I'm sure you've had a very tough go of it.

WALTER: Look: I know there's nothing we can do about last year, except put it behind us.

DAD: What are you suggesting?

WALTER: That maybe it's not too late.

DAD: For what?

WALTER: The tree's still down the basement, isn't it? In one of the boxes? I'll go down and bring it up. We can still have Christmas!

DAD: I wish it were that simple.

WALTER: What could be more simple?

DAD: There are complications with the assembly of the tree. You see, the colours on the tips of the branches wore off years ago. You do remember the colour-coding scheme on the tips of the branches, don't you Walter?

WALTER: I'm not sure.

DAD: The tree was assembled by sticking the ends of the branches into holes along the trunk. No great mystery there. Trouble was, there were many different sizes of branches. The big ones at the bottom, the little ones at the top. You've seen Christmas trees. I think the big ones were black, the little ones white. Obviously no one's going to mix up a white and a black. But the middle ones! The difference wasn't as obvious. A yellow and an orange can look pretty much the same to the untrained eye, let me tell you.

After years of normal use, these little drops of paint simply wore off the ends of the branches. I'd get the big ones into the bottom of the pole, no problem, but then I'd have a pile of branches without the foggiest notion of where they were supposed to go. Your mother would be whistling away, changing the burned-out lights in the string, without a care in the world. I just stood there, clutching these stupid branches, searching for traces of the paint to guide me in the assembly. Year after year it got worse. The colours were vanishing, and I was left with this sickening feeling that my life was vanishing with them. All the things I held dear to me, my work, my children – vanishing into the clear blue sky without a trace.

·I came to dread Christmas because of that tree. Not just the tree. But the other stuff. The cards that don't come in the mail. The meals that aren't cooked. The children who stay away.

He regards WALTER, *who averts his gaze.*

So, rather than go through all of that stress, rather than risk having an ungainly tree in the house, your mother and I decided we would have no tree. It's just safer all around.

WALTER: Safer?

DAD: Safer. Christmas can be a very treacherous time of year, son.

WALTER: (*Slight pause*) What about buying a real tree?

DAD: A real tree?!?!? And have needles all over the house?! Is that what you want?! Needles all over the house?

WALTER: Just a suggestion, is all.

DAD: Think about someone other than yourself for once!

WALTER: Sorry.

Pause.

WALTER: So, bottom line: no Christmas.

DAD: Your mother and I assumed we would simply pass the time like any other day. But now you and Gordon have come slinking back home....

WALTER: Gordon? Gordon came back home?

DAD: Yes.

WALTER: Is he still here?

DAD: Oh yeah. He's still here all right.

WALTER: Where?

DAD: Down the basement.

WALTER: What's *he* doing down the basement?

DAD: How would I know? All I can say is that he came charging through here a couple of days ago carrying some cardboard boxes and some supplies from Kenny's.

WALTER: I don't believe this! Gordon down the basement! Brother!

DAD: Yes, we have quite a full house all of a sudden. Gordon down the basement. You and me out here. Your mother in her room.

WALTER: Mom's in her room, is she?

DAD: Oh yes.

WALTER: Hmmm. How long's she been in there?

DAD: A while, a while.

WALTER: So, what is she doing in her room, exactly?

DAD: The Condition!

WALTER: The Condition! Jeez!

DAD: It comes and it stays. Dr. Bob has given it many different names over the years. And he's given your mother many, many different drugs and potions. I don't know anymore. I'm making hourly observations and recording them in my notebook. I have no doubt that your unexpected visit will cheer her up some.

WALTER: You're not suggesting I go in there!

DAD: She's your mother.

WALTER: But the Condition?!

DAD: It's Christmas. Walter. Reach down inside yourself and find the essence of the son she always hoped for. March right into that room, into the teeth of the Condition! Instead of just stumbling around like an insurance adjuster.

WALTER: It still burns you up, doesn't it?

DAD: I offered you the opportunity to sell the one thing responsible for the domestication of the Prairie West: barbed wire. All of my contacts, all of my leads. A business pioneered by my grandfather, passed down to his son, passed down to me. But you walked away from it. And for what?

WALTER: There's nothing wrong with insurance.

DAD: I have always thought of insurance as the self-fulfilling prophecy of the doomed.

WALTER: That's not fair.

DAD: You keep your house in order, and there's no need for insurance. And yet the glass towers keep on being erected, every pane of glass a window into the confused and wretched hearts of the policy holders.

WALTER: It's how I make my living, Dad. I'm sorry. My heart just wasn't in barbed wire. What can I say?

DAD: (*Handing him the flashlight*) There's nothing to say. Get in there and visit your mother.

WALTER: OK....

DAD: If you find her unconscious, perhaps you should tell me.

WALTER: Unconscious? What do you mean?

DAD: Immersed in a deep, profound sleep.

WALTER: Sleeping's one thing. But unconscious?

DAD: Always a possibility. The pharmaceuticals....

WALTER: What if she is? What'll we do?

DAD: Well, I'll begin by making a notation in my notebook. After that, I don't know. What would you suggest?

WALTER: Call 911?

DAD: 911?

WALTER: 911. The emergency number.

DAD: 911. Hmmm. That's good. That's very good. 911. I'll just make a note of that: 911. Good. Thank you, Walter.

WALTER: You're welcome.

DAD: Good luck.

WALTER *crosses the stage. As he does so, the light fades on* DAD.

SCENE THREE

Again the stage is dark. WALTER *enters* MOTHER'*s room, stumbles about in the dark. Finally, he turns the flashlight on.*

MOTHER: Gordon?

WALTER: No ... it's me. Walter.

MOTHER: Oh. Walter. What are you doing here?

WALTER: Just visiting.

MOTHER: Don't you dare shine that thing in my eyes.

WALTER: Sorry.

MOTHER: Turn it right off.

WALTER: (*Turning the flashlight off*) OK. OK.

MOTHER: Shhhh!

WALTER: Sorry.

MOTHER: You're loud. Much too loud.

WALTER: Sorry.

They sit in the darkness, in silence, for a moment.

MOTHER: The darkness has a liquid quality to it, fluid somehow. Sometimes, lying here, I feel like I'm on a raft, floating. (*Slight pause*) Give me some water, will you?

WALTER: (*Knocking over the stool he's been sitting on*) Sure, Mom.

MOTHER: In the jug. On the table.

WALTER: I just can't see to ... I'm going to have to turn the flashlight on to see what I'm doing here. Hide your eyes.

He turns the flashlight on, and at the same time lights come up very faintly on the bedroom. He pours water into the glass, and helps her drink.

WALTER: There you go.

MOTHER: Ahhh. I get so dry, especially at night. That's what happens, Walter, when you grow old. You dry up and you disappear. I can't stand the thought of getting up and walking out to the living room. I just can't see myself anymore.

Pause.

WALTER: Mom, I'm sorry I didn't get back to see you the last little while.

MOTHER: Two years.

WALTER: Is it really?

MOTHER: Two years ... long, long years.

WALTER: Boy. The time just flies, eh?

MOTHER: It creeps. Relentlessly, it creeps. It was Taffy, wasn't it?

WALTER: What?

MOTHER: The reason you stayed away so long: Taffy.

WALTER: I wouldn't say that.

MOTHER: Where is Taffy?

WALTER: She's not here.

MOTHER: The problem, Walter, is that we're not good enough for Taffy. Taffy with her Hair, and her Sweaters, and her Causes. Two years ago it was literacy. What is it now?

WALTER: Hunger.

MOTHER: Hunger. How satisfying that must be for Taffy.

WALTER: But it's not true, what you said.

MOTHER: What?

WALTER: That she's better than you. Or that she thinks....

MOTHER: In her mind it is. I'm sure it's easier for you to stay away.

WALTER: I'm sorry.

Pause.

WALTER: Can I get you anything? Some water?

MOTHER: (*Overlapping*) Water.

WALTER: Water. Coming right up.

MOTHER: So dry, so dry ...

Pause. He helps her drink.

MOTHER: All this water I drink, you'd think I'd just float away from here. Yet my mouth is filled with dust.

WALTER: You'll be OK, Mom. It's just the drugs....

MOTHER: It's no use, Walter. Everything has faded. Faded to grey. We're old, we're grey. Don't waste your time on us. Go back to Taffy.

WALTER: There's something I have to tell you about that, Mom.

MOTHER: I'm not up to it.

WALTER: But Mom....

MOTHER: Shhhhhh!

WALTER: Sorry!

MOTHER: You're loud. Much too loud.

WALTER: Sorry.

MOTHER: And clumsy.

WALTER: Yes, I know.

MOTHER: You exhaust me.

WALTER: I exhaust you?

MOTHER: Yes.

WALTER: I'm sorry.

MOTHER: You're not at all what I was expecting. Leave!

WALTER: OK, Mom.

MOTHER: Leave now!

WALTER: (*Bumping into the stool*) Yes, I will.

MOTHER: Shhh!

WALTER: Merry Christmas, Mom.

MOTHER: Just leave!

WALTER: I'm leaving!

Fade on bedroom.

SCENE FOUR

Lights come up on DAD *in living room area.* WALTER *enters and looks at* DAD, *who is writing small numbers in a pocket-sized notebook. Dean Martin is still crooning, quite loudly now.*

DAD: Conscious?

WALTER: Oh yes.

DAD: Nothing out of the usual, then?

WALTER: She seemed in pretty good spirits, actually. Quite jolly.

DAD: That's good.

Pause, as the music drones on.

WALTER: What is this, Dad? Dean Martin?!

DAD: Album #191: *Dean Martin's Greatest Hits.* It's Dean's turn in the Rotation.

WALTER: That's good. We certainly wouldn't want to hear any Christmas music.

DAD: You mock the Rotation. You, Gordon, Stacy. All of you mock the Rotation. But I think you'll find more and more as you grow older that one needs a system, one needs to impose order on the seething whirlpool of confusion and chaos swirling around us, or go mad. Mad, I say.

WALTER: If you've taught me anything, Dad, it's the importance of systems.

DAD: I'm pleased to hear that, son.

WALTER: The trouble is that you take your systems too far. They start controlling you.

DAD: Which is what systems are for. Protection from the raging current of primal instinct.

WALTER: But you don't even hear the music. You just check off the records in your little notebook and it's on to the next one.

DAD: #192: *One Hundred and One Strings Plays Beloved Excerpts From Carmen.*

WALTER: Whatever.

DAD: So what's your point?

WALTER: Forget it. I don't know why I bother.

The sound of an electric drill can be heard, faintly. (If GORDON is visible, he can be seen mixing up some eggnog.)

DAD: Shhh! Did you hear that?

WALTER: What?

DAD: It's Gordon.

WALTER: What's he doing?

DAD: Shhh! Listen!

They listen. The drill is heard again.

DAD: He's playing with my Makita!

The drill pulses a couple of times, then all is silent from the basement again.

WALTER: So, he's really down there.

DAD: Oh yes, he's down there, all right. I can hear him moving around, dragging things across the floor. Sometimes at night, I hear him crying.

WALTER: Crying?! That's terrible.

DAD: It certainly is.

WALTER: Can't you do something?

DAD: I tried to go down, once. But he threatened to shoot me.

WALTER: He's armed?

DAD: And dangerous.

WALTER: You can't be serious!

DAD: I'm dead serious.

WALTER: I don't know why I thought things would be any different.

WALTER *goes to get his coat, preparing to leave.*

DAD: What are you doing?

WALTER: I'm leaving, I guess.

DAD: You just got here.

WALTER: And now I'm going.

WALTER *puts on his coat and boots.*

DAD: This is certainly not what I had in mind when I was a young man and saw the elk.

WALTER: What elk?

DAD: I saw an elk kicking at the ground, twisting his neck, rolling his eyes and sniffing the crisp mountain air. That's when I knew.

WALTER: Knew what?

DAD: That I had to be like the elk, had to become the elk. Turn over the stones on my territory. Take a female, increase the population of the herd. The rest is history. Your mother. You and Gordon and Stacy. The herd continues to prosper, in a limited sort of way.

WALTER: Where did you see this elk?

DAD: I saw the elk on *Mutual of Omaha's Wild Kingdom*.

WALTER: With what's his name ...

DAD: Marlin Perkins.

WALTER: ... Marlin Perkins.

DAD: That is correct. A naturalist, and a gentleman.

WALTER: And Woody Woodpecker.

DAD: Yes, good old Woody. Marlin and Woody. They were adept at probing the essence of the primal instincts.

WALTER: Primal instincts, right!

DAD: Don't ever underestimate the lure of the primal instincts, son. Despite what you might think, Mr. Insurance Adjuster, there's a lot to be learned from Marlin Perkins, and people of his . . . i(e)lk.

WALTER: I saw something about *Wild Kingdom* on TV one night.

DAD: Is that right?

WALTER: Claimed that Marlin Perkins was a fraud.

DAD: No he wasn't!

WALTER: Said the program was a sham.

DAD: How dare you say that?

WALTER: It was staged. They drugged the animals. Threw them together and let them fight it out on film.

DAD: Don't ever say that!

WALTER: It's all been documented, Dad. I'm not making this up.

DAD: You're sailing on some very dangerous waters here, son.

WALTER: I'm sure I am. Listen, Dad ... maybe some other time. I can't deal with all this right now....

DAD *rears back and makes the woeful bellow of the bull elk.*

WALTER: What are you doing?

DAD: That's the woeful bellow of the bull elk, my boy.

He rears back and bellows again.

DAD: Kind of makes the blood run, doesn't it? There comes a time, Walter, in the life of the bull elk, when a younger, stronger male challenges him to become leader of the herd.

WALTER: What are you saying?

DAD: I'm saying it's time for you to throw your head back and roar! I'm saying it's time for you to take charge. Sharpen your horns against the rocks. Make things happen. Instead of just slinking off into the night ....

WALTER: I'm not slinking off into the night....

DAD: Try it.

WALTER: Try what?

DAD: Throw your head back and roar. *Roaaaaaar!*

WALTER: It's no use, Dad.

DAD: *Roaaaaaar!* Come on.

WALTER: (*Quiet, embarrassed*) roar....

DAD: *Roaaaaaar!*

WALTER: ... roarrrr ....

They roar back and forth until DAD *is satisfied.*

DAD: Not bad.

WALTER: What do you want from me?

DAD: What do you want, Walter? What are you looking for?

WALTER: I don't know. I honestly don't know. I don't even know where to begin looking....

DAD: You can begin by going down the basement.

WALTER: But Gordon's down there!

DAD: That's the point! He's your little brother.

WALTER: (*Taking off his coat*) Why me?

DAD: You're the oldest.

WALTER: Oh, brother.

DAD: No one asks to be the oldest, Walter. No one in their right mind would choose to be first born. When I think of the mistakes your mother and I made with you....When you get down there, make special notice of my barbed wire samples. I suppose I can replace the power tools if I have to. But you know what that wire means to me, Walter.

WALTER: It was your life, once.

DAD: (*Overlapping*) It was my life, once. Why, your grandfather and I opened up the whole Cypress Hills area.

WALTER: Opened it up by fencing everything in.

DAD: It put meat on our table.

WALTER: (*Overlapping*) It put meat on our table.

Pause.

WALTER: Well, I'll go down, then.

DAD: Good luck, son. And be careful.

WALTER: Right.

WALTER *leaves the living room and goes to the top of the stairs. Lights fade on living room.*

SCENE FIVE

Lights come up fully on the basement. Although it is an unfinished basement, GORDON *has been making it his home for the last little while. He has fashioned a bit of a living area in the concrete. An area rug, book shelves. A few paintings hang from the wall. Crudely. Clothes everywhere, including socks and underwear that hang from a clothes line made from barbed wire. Power tools everywhere. An Elvis bust. Along one of the walls, vast numbers of cardboard boxes, all neatly stacked and labelled. Spilling out of a few of these boxes are some children's toys, vestiges of Christmases past, including a number of Barbie dolls showing evidence of mutilation and torture. There is also an arsenal of toy weaponry – various water pistols, toy six-gun and holster outfits, and a Johnny 7 multipurpose gun, capable of firing a number of different projectiles.*

Beside the boxes and the toys are a number of spools of barbed wire. There is an easy chair with a trilight beside it, and an old hide-a-bed. In the centre of the living area, on a blue steamer trunk, is a crystal bowl filled with eggnog.

GORDON *is in his chair, reading* A Christmas Carol. *He has an afghan wrapped around his shoulders, as it is obviously cold and damp in the basement. Beside him, he has a BB gun, the classic Daisy 22 model.*

WALTER: *(From the top of the stairs)* Gordon?

GORDON *tenses, and grabs the gun. Before* WALTER *comes down,* GORDON *hides the gun under the afghan.*

Hello? You down there, Gordon?

GORDON: Who's that?

WALTER: It's me: Walter!

GORDON: Is that you, Walter?

WALTER: Yeah, it's me.

Pause.

GORDON: What do you want?

WALTER: Can I come down?

GORDON: What for?

WALTER: To visit?

GORDON: Are you alone?

WALTER: Yes.

Pause.

GORDON: Come on down.

WALTER *enters, taking it all in with mild disgust.*

WALTER: Hello, Gordon.

GORDON: Hello, Walter.

WALTER: Merry Christmas.

GORDON: Yeah, right.

Pause.

WALTER: So ... another year, eh?

GORDON: What's that supposed to mean?!

WALTER: Nothing, Gordon. Relax.

GORDON: I am relaxed!

WALTER: You don't seem relaxed.

GORDON: Well, I am.

Pause.

WALTER: So ... just the two of us down here on Christmas Eve, eh? Funny thing....

GORDON: What's so funny about it?

WALTER: Oh, I don't know. The shifting fortunes of man, or something. (*Noticing the punch bowl*) Say ... you've got eggnog down here?

GORDON: What about it?

WALTER: Always been one of my favorite Christmas beverages. Yes sir. I do look forward to Christmas for the eggnog, if for nothing else.

Long pause.

GORDON: You want one?

WALTER: Sure, I'll have an eggnog. What would Christmas be without a little eggnog? It's not that processed stuff though, is it?

GORDON: No.

WALTER: That's good.... You gotta watch that processed stuff, keep your eye on the best-before date.... Once the best-before date has lapsed, you're on your own.

GORDON: Is that right?

WALTER: You're darned tootin'.

GORDON: I've never paid much attention to those things.

WALTER: Have you ever had food poisoning, Gordon?

GORDON: Gee, Walter. I don't think I have.

WALTER: You don't think you have?

GORDON: No. I don't think so.

WALTER: It's not one of those things you quickly forget, Gordon. Either you've had food poisoning or you haven't.

GORDON: OK. I've never had it.

WALTER: So you don't know what it's like.

GORDON: I guess not.

WALTER: It's like the human body is trying to turn itself inside out.

GORDON: Is that a fact?

WALTER: Oh, yes. You discover the vilest jellies and juices, stuff you were never meant to see, or smell, or taste. All kinds of things, erupting from deep within your body, gushing out both ends at the same time. You'd better hope you have a sink and a toilet in close proximity if you ever get yourself a dose of food poisoning.

GORDON: Sounds rough.

WALTER: Rough doesn't begin to cover it.

GORDON: (*Handing* WALTER *a glass of eggnog*) Well, I made this eggnog myself, and I've been drinking it for days now, and my body hasn't tried to turn itself inside out so I think it's probably safe.

WALTER: No MSG?

GORDON: No. Do you need some?

WALTER: No. I shun MSG.

GORDON: Well, there's no MSG in this eggnog. This eggnog is the real thing.

WALTER: Kind of strange texture, there Gord. How'd you make it?

GORDON: The normal way.

WALTER: What do you consider to be the normal way?

GORDON: Mix up the rum and the eggs. Add a bit of nutmeg.

WALTER: Hmmmm. Just the rum and the eggs, eh?

GORDON: Yeah.

WALTER: No milk?

GORDON: No. But nutmeg.

WALTER: How unusual.

GORDON: There's no law saying you have to have milk in eggnog, is there?

WALTER: No. Thousands of recipes suggest it, but probably no laws say you actually have to have it ... unfortunately.

GORDON: I don't mind it without milk.

WALTER: Eggnog with no milk.

GORDON: It's not called milknog. It's called eggnog. Eggs are the crucial element. Not to mention the rum.

WALTER: True. But I always thought milk was a pretty crucial element, too. Critical, even.

GORDON: OK. I'm going to level with you Walter.

WALTER: What?

GORDON: I've run out of milk. A while back. At first it worried me, but I got used to it. Just one less thing to worry about. So there you have it.

WALTER: Back up a second, Gordon. You say you worried about the milk.

GORDON: Yeah?

WALTER: Were you worried about the milk, or were you worried about the fact that you ran out of milk?

GORDON: Both, I guess.

WALTER: OK. Let's take this one step at a time, shall we?

GORDON: Take what?

WALTER: The milk situation. You worried about the milk, when in fact there was milk down here to worry about. Is that right?

GORDON: Well, there's no fridge down here. So I had to – you know – sniff it before drinking it.

WALTER: OK. I can see that. Smell check on the milk. Very prudent. What about the eggs?

GORDON: What about the eggs?

WALTER: How can the eggs keep if the milk can't?

GORDON: It's cool enough down here for the eggs.

WALTER: Not cool enough for milk, but cool enough for eggs?

GORDON: Yeah.

WALTER: What kind of system do you use to monitor your eggs?

GORDON: Huh?!?!

WALTER: What kinds of checks and balances do you have in place to ensure the freshness of your eggs?

GORDON: I don't have a system for my eggs.

WALTER: You don't have a system for your eggs.

GORDON: Are you telling me you have a system for your eggs?

WALTER: Yes. I write the date on my eggs.

GORDON: What?

WALTER: On the shell, with a nontoxic felt marker.

GORDON: You're so much like the old man, Walter, it's frightening. Writing on your eggs. Wow!

WALTER: You can say what you like, but I firmly believe we need systems to regulate our lives. And we certainly need to know, beyond the shadow of a doubt, that the foods we ingest are fresh and free from contamination. You've never had food poisoning, so you don't understand how critical this all is.

GORDON: Walter. The eggs are fine.

WALTER: Hmmmmffff.

GORDON: I'm living down here and I know what keeps and what doesn't keep and I'm telling you the eggs are fine, Walter. OK?

WALTER: I guess so.

GORDON: So cheers, OK?

WALTER: OK. Cheers.

GORDON *raises his glass and takes a big drink.* WALTER *sniffs at his glass suspiciously, is about to drink but changes his mind at the last minute.*

WALTER: There's just the rum and eggs in here?

GORDON: And a bit of nutmeg.

WALTER: Look, why don't I run upstairs and get some milk?

GORDON: No!

WALTER: Why not?

GORDON: They've got their stuff, I've got mine. That's just the way it's got to be. If I need milk, I'll run over to Kenny's and get it myself.

WALTER: Why don't you then?

GORDON: I don't feel much like going out right now. There could be carollers out there!

WALTER: I could run over to Kenny's.

GORDON: Forget it. Look: I want to see you drink the eggnog!

WALTER: I don't know if I can drink it like this, Gordon.

GORDON: Please, Walter!

WALTER: I don't know.

GORDON: I beg of you, just drink the eggnog, OK?

WALTER: Just like this?

GORDON: Yeah.

WALTER: Just as she comes.

GORDON: Yeah.

WALTER: Just the rum and eggs.

GORDON: Just drink the eggnog, OK?!?!?!

WALTER: OK.

GORDON: Cheers!

WALTER: Cheers.

GORDON *drinks, but just as* WALTER *is about to sip his glass, he notices the punch bowl.*

WALTER: Saaaaaay ... that punch bowl.

GORDON: Aw, for crying out loud!

WALTER: Eh?

GORDON: What?

WALTER: That's it, is it?

GORDON: Yeah.

WALTER: The one I gave you for a wedding present. .

GORDON: Yeah.

WALTER: Well, isn't that something. She's standing up pretty well, eh?

GORDON: Yeah.

WALTER: Sometimes it's worth paying that little bit extra.

GORDON: Well, that punch bowl doesn't owe me a thing, that's for sure. (*Picks up the gun, aims it at* WALTER'*s head.*) Now drink your eggnog before I blow your eyeball out of your head.

WALTER: Sure, Gord. Sure. Just put the gun down, will you?

GORDON: *Drink the eggnog!!!!!!*

WALTER: OK, OK, OK.

GORDON: Cheers!

WALTER: Cheers.

Pause as they both drink. GORDON *lowers the gun.*

GORDON: Well?

WALTER: Hmm. Viscous.

GORDON: But not bad, eh?

WALTER: It's a texture thing, Gordon. Like taking a sip from a spittoon: once you get started, it's hard to stop.

GORDON: But the taste?

WALTER: The taste isn't bad. I'll give you that.

GORDON: (*Raising his glass*) Cheers.

WALTER: Cheers.

They drink again as lights fade on the basement.

Scene Six

MOTHER'*s room.* DAD *is sitting in a chair beside her bed with the flashlight on.*

DAD: Nice to have Walter home.

MOTHER: Is it?

DAD: Sure. We had a nice talk.

MOTHER: Did you?

DAD: We certainly did.

MOTHER: Any sign of Gordon?

DAD: No.

MOTHER: What can he be doing down there?!

DAD: I'm not sure. Walter's joined him down there.

MOTHER: Can he draw Gordon out, do you think?

DAD: Those two have always had a special knack for communicating. If anyone can draw Gordon out, I think it would be Walter.

MOTHER: Then....

DAD: What?

MOTHER: Nothing.

DAD: No.

MOTHER: I was going to say, although I know you don't want to hear it – but if Gordon can be drawn out, and as Walter is here anyway, don't you think we should be making some kind of plans?

DAD: No.

MOTHER: You don't.

DAD: I think it's premature to be making plans.

MOTHER: Premature.

DAD: Yes.

MOTHER: So, still no tree.

DAD: That's right.

MOTHER: Not to mention the yule log and stockings and manger scene and all the other stuff.

DAD: Right again.

MOTHER: Premature.

Pause.

MOTHER: I think there may be a turkey in the deep freeze.

DAD: I don't want to hear about it.

MOTHER: If it's not a turkey, it's a big enough chicken....

DAD: Which is exactly where it will stay: in the deep freeze.

MOTHER: Yes, I believe it is a big chicken. A big, succulent free-range chicken I bought from the Hutterites. And I think there may be a bag of brussel sprouts in there as well....

DAD: Never mind the brussel sprouts....

MOTHER: Of course, the chicken will have to be thawed, which means you'll have to set it in water....

DAD: I'm not doing it, Charlotte.

MOTHER: Why not?

DAD: Those two are as likely to end up in a bar somewhere watching obscure bowl games as spending any time with us. I could go out there right now and find they've left already. Then it's you and me staring across the turkey at each other.

MOTHER: Chicken.

DAD: Turkey, chicken, it doesn't matter. I won't have anything to do with it.

MOTHER: Why?

DAD: Because I'm always the one who has to mop up. I'm the one who has to call Doctor Bob. I'm the one who has to go out to the pharmacy for another bottle of pills. Don't just lie there torturing yourself with hope. Shut it off for awhile. Get some real rest.

MOTHER: Yes, dear.

DAD: Not another thought about the big chicken.

MOTHER: The furthest thing from my mind.

He leaves. Lights fade on MOTHER.

SCENE SEVEN

DAD *returns to the living room. Like a ghost,* STACY *is standing by the front door, wearing a flannel nightgown and Phentex slippers. Her hair is, to say the least, highly unusual.*

STACY: Hello, Daddy.

DAD: Stacy!! Where on earth did you come from?

STACY: You know where I've come from. No big secret there.

DAD: I suppose not. But when....

STACY: Just today. I've managed to turn the page. I know that might seem hard to believe. After the solvent ... and the pinking shears. But I've put all that behind me. And turned the page.

DAD: Well, isn't that something!

STACY: Daddy?

DAD: Yes, dear?

STACY: You don't have a cigarette, do you?

DAD: No. Sorry.

STACY: Do you think there might be some, anywhere in the house?

DAD: I doubt it. There's always Kenny's.

STACY: I don't feel much like going out there again....

DAD: Well, come in....

STACY: I'm not interrupting anything?

DAD: Just monitoring the Rotation.

STACY: Oh yeah....

DAD: But it can wait, I suppose. Sit down.

Pause. She sits with some obvious difficulty in his recliner.

STACY: I was tooling a leather belt. I've gotten pretty good at it. I suddenly realized there's no great mystery to any of this. In fact, when you get right down to it, it's not mysterious at all. It's terribly ordinary, really. Have you ever felt that? That everything's just terribly ordinary?

DAD: Yes, I think I've felt that. I think everyone feels it, sooner or later.

STACY: Really?

DAD: I think so.

STACY: Do you think that even if everything is terribly ordinary, that something special can still happen?

DAD: I don't know if I'd hold my breath on that one....

Pause.

STACY: Where's Mom?

DAD: In her room.

STACY: Oh. How long's she been there?

DAD: Oh, a while. A while.

STACY: What's she doing there?

DAD: Not much.

STACY: Oh boy!

DAD: Yeah.

STACY: What brought that on?

DAD: The Festive Season, I guess.

STACY: I hate it. Suicides are way up. Domestic violence. Substance abuse. You might as well crawl under your bed and ride it out.

Pause.

DAD: So, maybe it wouldn't be such a bad idea for you to pop in and say hello?

STACY: She doesn't want company.

DAD: Come on now, honey.

STACY: Aw, Daddy.

DAD: She is your mother.

STACY: I know.

DAD: She grunted and sweated to get you into the world.

STACY: I know.

DAD: The least you can do is pop in and say hello.

STACY: I just don't feel much like popping in there.

DAD: A little visit from you might be just the ticket to cheer her up a bit.

STACY: I don't think she wants to see me. You remember the last time....

DAD: Well, now, little one. Sometimes your mother gets feeling a little bit ... down. As do we all. Sometimes things are said in the heat of the moment we all wish we could take back.

STACY: I don't think I can go in there tonight, Daddy.

DAD: No?

STACY: We'll only fight. I didn't come home to fight. Not at Christmas....

DAD *gets up and crosses over to the stereo. He puts on a pair of white cotton gloves and removes Dean Martin from the turntable.*

DAD: Suit yourself. You can always stay out here with Dad and listen to some records.

STACY: Oh yeah....

DAD: It gets a little bit lonely, sitting out here monitoring the Rotation all by myself.

STACY: I'm sure it does.

DAD: Coming up we have one of your favourites.

STACY: We do?

DAD: Good old Album #192: *101 Strings Plays Beloved Excerpts From Carmen.* (*He hums some of the overture for her*)

STACY: I think maybe I'll take my chances with Mom.

DAD: That's too bad.

STACY: I'm sure she needs company.

DAD: Shine the flashlight into her eyes. If her pupils don't contract for some reason, let me know and we'll call 911, OK?

STACY: Yes, Daddy.

She leaves. DAD *takes out his pen and conducts the overture to Carmen. Slow fade on living room.*

Scene Eight

Lights up on GORDON *and* WALTER *in the basement.*

GORDON: Great! *Carmen*! His bloody system is going to drive me insane. It's ordered chaos is all it is. It's one giant oxymoron.

WALTER: Like jumbo shrimp.

GORDON: Exactly.

WALTER: Like military intelligence.

GORDON: Yes. I jussss....

WALTER: Like *Little Big Man.*

GORDON: Right....

WALTER: Like Richie Rich, Poor Little Rich Boy.

GORDON: Looks like you've got the oxymoron thing pretty well covered there, Walter.

WALTER: Figures of speech have always been a big favourite of mine.

GORDON: I don't think I ever knew that about you.

WALTER: Oh yes. Metaphor ... simile ... conceit ... I know them all. But oxymoron holds a special place in my heart.

GORDON: Is this something that comes up a lot in the insurance business? Figures of speech?

WALTER: People expect a lot of their adjustor. I make it my business to know how things work, and I include language in that. Anyway....

Pause.

WALTER: So ... what's going on, Gord?

GORDON: What do you mean?

WALTER: You're holed up down the folks' basement. You're armed.

GORDON: I don't want to talk about it.

WALTER: Where's Carla?

GORDON: *Carlene.*

WALTER: Carlene. Sorry.

GORDON: I don't want to talk about it.

WALTER: OK. That's OK. We don't have to talk about it.

GORDON: Good, 'cause I don't want to.

WALTER: No problem. We can just sit here and listen to *Carmen.*

Long pause.

GORDON: She took off. Up north. With a bush pilot.

WALTER: Wow!

GORDON: I don't know what it is now, Walter. But I don't feel comfortable out there. Everyone's talking about it.

WALTER: About what?

GORDON: You know. Carlene, the bush pilot ... me.

WALTER: Who's talking about it?

GORDON: The people in the malls. In restaurants. I can hear them, sometimes. They stop talking when I get in range.

WALTER: If they stop talking when you get in range, how do you know they're talking about you?

GORDON: I can tell by the way they look at me. I know they know. They take one look at me and they know. Even Kenny knows.

WALTER: What?

GORDON: That I blew it. Despite all my potential, no one will have me.

WALTER: I think you're being a little hard on yourself there, Gordon.

GORDON: You just don't know what it's like. I envy you for that.

WALTER: For what?

GORDON: You're kind of an old-fashioned man, Walter.

WALTER: What's that supposed to mean?

GORDON: Well, you've got a job. You put on a tie and drive to work. You come home and have a martini, I'd imagine. Taffy has supper ready. After supper you watch TV. Or read. You're not sitting in your shorts staring at the clock, wondering where your wife is. She's right there beside you. Or out in the kitchen, ironing. You go to bed, get up the next morning, do it all again.

WALTER: In fact – Never mind. This isn't so bad, once you get on to it.

GORDON: You want another one?

WALTER: Why not? We can drink some milk later.

GORDON *cracks three eggs into the crystal bowl and pours in half a bottle of rum. Fade to black as he prepares to stir this with a contraption he has constructed by fitting a few loops of barbed wire into a three-speed cordless rechargeable reversible Makita hand drill.*

SCENE NINE

The stage is in momentary blackness. MOTHER *is sitting up in the gurney, sipping on a glass of water. Suddenly,* STACY's *face emerges from the shadows, illuminated by the flashlight. Throughout this scene, the Makita can be heard from time to time, a cordless handheld chorus, commenting on the action in the bedroom.*

STACY: Mother?

MOTHER: Stacy!? Is it really you?

STACY: Yes. In the flesh. If I can use that word.

MOTHER: What word?

STACY: Flesh. You know, after last time....

MOTHER: Why don't we just put that behind us and start over again, shall we?

STACY: I'd like that.

MOTHER: You look like a phantom, dancing around in that stupid light of your father's. Turn on the light and let me see you.

Lights come up on the bedroom. They embrace. MOTHER *strokes* STACY's *hair a few times. The hug turns into an examination of her hair.*

MOTHER: It's good to have you home again, baby. Hmm....

STACY: What?

MOTHER: Nothing, dear. Nothing at all. Sit down. I want to hear everything that's happened to you since I saw you last.

STACY: In a second. Why did you go "Hmm"?

MOTHER: It was just the sound you make when you're giving someone a hug.

STACY: I know the sound of a hug. This was something else, like something occurred to you.

Pause. Drill.

MOTHER: When you were little, you had hair you could sit on. We brushed it 101 times every night. It broke my heart, the first time we cut your hair.

STACY: Is there's something wrong with my hair?

MOTHER: It seems rather dull, somehow. Lacklustre.

STACY: Lacklustre?!?!

MOTHER: I shouldn't have said anything.

STACY: Lacklustre!

Pause. Drill.

MOTHER: Jojoba!

STACY: What about it?

MOTHER: It imparts a healthy sheen. You need something with jojoba.

STACY: I've got something with sea plasma.

MOTHER: It's not working.

STACY: It's supposed to be good.

MOTHER: It may be good, but it's not working. Anyone can see that. Get yourself something with jojoba and you'll be a lot further ahead. If you need money, I'll be happy to give it to you.

STACY: I don't need money, and I don't need jojoba, and I don't need you passing judgement on me every time I walk in here. Look at your hair! Look at your life! Who the hell are you to talk about lacklustre?!

MOTHER: That's enough!

STACY: I don't mind not finding anything special. I don't even mind not finding a Christmas tree. But I do mind coming back after fourteen months and having you insult my hair! That really hurts, Mother. It really sucks the big one.

MOTHER: Don't talk to me that way!

STACY: You don't like it, get up and do something about it instead of lying there all day.

MOTHER: You think I like lying here?

STACY: Yes.

MOTHER: You think I choose this?

STACY: I do.

MOTHER: Get out!

STACY: I'm getting. Merry Christmas!

She leaves. Slow fade on MOTHER *in bed.*

SCENE TEN

Lights up on basement. GORDON *and* WALTER *are sipping their eggnog, picking up from the end of Scene Eight.*

GORDON: The point is, Walter, you rule your roost. You feel like taking off Christmas eve to check out the old homestead, you just do it. That's what I meant by being old-fashioned. I meant it in a good sense. Where is Taffy, anyway?

WALTER: Working, I guess.

GORDON: On Christmas Eve?

WALTER: Always working ... always working.... Very ambitious woman, Taffy. Have you thought of going after her?

GORDON: No. I wouldn't even know where to begin. She could be anywhere. Where do bush pilots fly?

WALTER: I don't know. In the bush. Above the bush.

GORDON: Up north.

WALTER: Definitely up north.

GORDON: I just get this cold, empty feeling when I think about it. Do you know that feeling?

WALTER: Unbroken expanses. Oh yes. I know the feeling.

Pause.

GORDON: Listen, Walter, it's been great seeing you. It's been nice. But I think I need to be alone now.

Pause.

So thanks for dropping in.

WALTER: I'm staying.

GORDON: Staying where? Staying here?

WALTER: That's right.

GORDON: Oh no, you're not.

WALTER: Why not?

GORDON: I've turned this into my personal living space and I'm not sharing it with anyone. I need the solitude.

WALTER: Solitude's the last thing you need. You're distraught.

GORDON: I am not!

WALTER: Yes you are.

GORDON: Why don't you just go back to your own family instead of hanging around here?

WALTER: I'm not leaving.

GORDON: (*Grabbing the gun*) I'm warning you, Walter. Get out of here before I do something we'll both regret.

WALTER: Put the gun down, Gordon!

GORDON: You've had your eggnog. There's nothing left for you down here. Now clear out.

WALTER: You're going to have to shoot me, Gordon. Because I'm not leaving.

GORDON: If that's the way you want it, brother. Say your prayers!

GORDON *cocks the gun. Very slight pause.*

WALTER: You know, if I didn't know better, I'd say that looks a lot like your old BB gun.

GORDON: You're saying this is a BB gun?

WALTER: Yeah. That's exactly what I'm saying. And I'll tell you something, Gordon. (WALTER *inches over and grabs his old Johnny 7*) No BB gun is any match for my Johnny 7!

He dives behind the couch. GORDON *takes cover behind some boxes.*

GORDON: I could still put your eye out with this thing!

WALTER: I could carve my initials in your forehead with this thing!

GORDON: Yeah, well I could put one up your nostril so far you couldn't reach it with a coat hanger!

WALTER: I could melt your fillings!

GORDON: This basement just ain't big enough for the two of us!

Quick blackout on basement.

Scene Eleven

STACY *returns to the living room. She walks right past* DAD *on her way to the front door.*

DAD: Did you and your mother have a nice visit, pumpkin?

STACY: We chatted.

DAD: What did you chat about?

STACY: Girl talk. You know. Daddy?

DAD: Yes, dear?

STACY: Does my hair seem lacklustre to you?

DAD: Noooooo ... I wouldn't say lacklustre.

STACY: Thank you.

DAD: A bit unkempt, dishevelled, but not necessarily lacklustre.

STACY: What is this with my hair?!

DAD: You asked.

STACY: I have to get out of here. I have to leave. What am I saying? Where do I have to go? I can't go out there. I don't even have a coat!

DAD: Everything OK, Stacy?

STACY: I need a moment to get myself together, Daddy.

DAD: Well, just make yourself at home. I'm just going to put on side two here of *Carmen*. This is one of my favorite spots in the Rotation. After *Carmen*, we have good old Album #193, *My Fair Lady*:

"And *Oh!* The towering fee-ling
"Just to know, somehow you are near...."
Beautiful stuff. Good old Rex and Julie.

STACY: Julie? Julie who?

DAD: Julie Andrews.

STACY: I thought it was Katherine Hepburn.

DAD: You mean Audrey.

STACY: Katherine, Audrey. Whatever.

DAD: It was Julie Andrews.

STACY: No way. I saw it.

DAD: You saw the movie.

STACY: Yeah?!

DAD: Album #193 is the original cast recording of the Broadway production. That had Julie in it. Not Audrey.

STACY: It might have been her acting, but that's not her on the record.

DAD: Of the Broadway musical, honey, it is.

STACY: But she didn't do her own singing.

DAD: Of course she did.

STACY: No she didn't. They had to bring in someone else to sing for her.

DAD: You're thinking of Audrey. Audrey didn't sing in the movie. They had to bring in Marni Nixon. But Julie definitely sang for herself.

STACY: But she didn't in the *Sound of Music*. They had to get some nun to sing for her.

DAD: Don't you think you're being a little unfair to Julie, little one?

STACY: Unfair to Julie?!

DAD: I'm sure she worked very hard, learning those songs, getting the nuances just so.

STACY: I don't give a rat's ass about Julie Andrews or Audrey Hepburn or any of them. What about me? What about caring about me?!

DAD: Now, now dear. At the moment, we're busy caring about the subset of women who have performed in *My Fair Lady*, which you don't belong to. On any account, there's no point arguing about it, is there? Album #193 is the original cast recording of the Broadway musical, with Rex and Julie, so let's just sit back and have a good listen. After *Carmen*, of course. We wouldn't want to shortchange *Carmen* now, would we?

STACY: What about shortchanging me?

DAD: No one's shortchanging you, dear.

STACY: You don't even know when you're doing it. I should have known better. Nothing good ever happens to me around here.

She goes to the door.

DAD: Stacy! I won't let you leave! Not like this. Not without a coat.

STACY: I don't have a coat, if you didn't notice.

DAD: Down the basement ... in one of the boxes. You'll find two cloth coats and an orange shaggy parka.

STACY: You kept my orange shaggy parka? What about the stain?

DAD: I'm sure the stain's faded by now, dear. It's 37 below out there. They say human flesh can freeze in thirty seconds....

STACY: OK, OK. I'll get my coat. But I'm not staying.

She leaves for the basement. Fade on living room.

Scene Twelve

Lights up on basement. GORDON *and* WALTER *as before.*

WALTER: Just for one night, Gordon. Just the two of us. What do you say?

GORDON: Where are you going to sleep?

WALTER: Where have you been sleeping?

GORDON: In the hide-a-bed.

WALTER: Then we'll sleep in the hide-a-bed.

GORDON: Together?

WALTER: Why not?

GORDON: There's not even room for one in that thing. I'm not getting in there with you.

WALTER: Why not?

GORDON: You're a thrasher. You fling your arms around and kick your legs like you're drowning.

WALTER: OK. Listen, Gordon I'll make a deal with you.

GORDON: What deal?

WALTER: You let me stay here with you tonight. We'll just get through Christmas, then I'll help you get your own place. I'll pay the rent until you get some cash together.

GORDON: You'd do that for me?

WALTER: Of course I would.

GORDON: Why?

WALTER: Because I'm your big brother.

GORDON *comes out.*

GORDON: OK, Walter. You can stay. Just don't touch any of my stuff.

WALTER: OK.

GORDON: I know it's not much, but it's the only stuff I've got.

WALTER: No problem. I tell you, it won't be long till we have you back on your feet. You can play the single life again.

GORDON: I wouldn't know how anymore.

WALTER: It's easy. You just need a water bed and some posters.

GORDON: That's the single life? A water bed and posters?

WALTER: Yeah.

GORDON: Brother....

WALTER: And of course you'll need some women.

GORDON: Forget it! I'm done with women. I don't care if I see another woman for as long as I live.

STACY *emerges from behind the boxes. The boys put their guns on her.*

WALTER: *Aighghghgh!*

GORDON: *(Overlapping) Aighghghgh!*

STACY: *(Overlapping) Aighghghgh!*

Quick blackout on entire stage.

END OF ACT ONE

ACT TWO

SCENE THIRTEEN

Flashlight comes on as in Scene One. MOM *is in the gurney with the covers pulled over her head.*

DAD: Hello?

MOTHER: Leave me alone.

DAD: Time for your medication. I must say I think this one is working quite well. Sit up now.

She sits up. He gives her pills and some water.

DAD: So, you and Stacy managed to have a nice little visit, did you?

MOTHER: I picked on her. She came in ready to make up and I picked on her. About her hair, of all things!

DAD: She's gone down the basement.

MOTHER: All our children ... down the basement.

DAD: At least this year we know where they are.

MOTHER: And poor Gordon won't have to spend Christmas alone down there.

DAD: Remember all those Christmas Eves we spent, putting all those contraptions together? The wagons and the doll houses and the tricycles and bicycles. No matter what I did, no matter how carefully I followed the instructions, there was always one screw left over. Or worse: I'd end up one screw short. Charlotte, maybe you were right.

MOTHER: About what?

DAD: The turkey. Or the big chicken or whatever it is....

MOTHER: Chicken.

DAD: ... and the brussel sprouts. Maybe we should put together a Christmas feast.

MOTHER: Do you think they'll stay?

DAD: It's pretty hard to resist the smell of a chicken cooking in the oven.

MOTHER: I don't know if I'm up to it.

DAD: I could help.

MOTHER: You've never cooked a chicken in your life.

DAD: It can't be that hard to assemble a fowl supper. What are the steps?

MOTHER: The chicken needs to be thawed. In cool water, left alone. No worrying it.

DAD: Sounds simple enough.

MOTHER: After that, well, it's a Hutterite chicken, so it would need to be cleaned properly.

DAD: It's eviscerated, isn't it?!

MOTHER: They may have missed a few things.

DAD: Like what?

MOTHER: You know. A lung. The liver. The heart. Although all that stuff should be wrapped in paper in the cavity.

DAD: What do I do?

MOTHER: Just take them out.

DAD: Reach my hand in there and draw them out.

MOTHER: But not until it's thawed.

DAD: And if I thawed it, you'd be inclined to cook it? Is that what I'm hearing?

MOTHER: If they're still here in the morning, and the chicken has thawed, then I'll see.

DAD: Then I'll go thaw the chicken. Anything you need?

MOTHER: Set it in cool water.

DAD: Cool water. Right.

MOTHER: And don't worry it.

DAD: I'll just let nature take it's course.

He leaves. Lights fade on MOTHER.

SCENE FOURTEEN

Lights come up on the basement. The same as at the end of scene twelve.

WALTER: *AIGHGHGHGH!*

GORDON: (*Overlapping*) *AIGHGHGHGH!*

STACY: (*Overlapping*) *AIGHGHGHGH!*

Slight break.

STACY: What are you guys doing down here?!!!!!

GORDON: What are you doing down here?!

STACY: And why are you carrying around guns?

GORDON: We were engaged in a Mexican standoff.

STACY: Well put it down. *Put them down! Right now!* It gives me the creeps. You could shoot someone with that thing.

GORDON: Couldn't it I wanted to: don't have any BBs left.

STACY: That's a BB gun?

GORDON: Yes.

STACY: You guys are pathetic. A couple of grown men walking around with toy guns. They put people away for far less deviant activity than that, let me tell you. When I look around and see the people who are still walking around the streets it makes me ... it makes me....

GORDON: Crazy?

STACY: Don't ever use that word around me, Gordon, if you know what's good for you. Don't use it. Don't even think it!

GORDON: Sorry.

STACY: Toy guns! Boy, am I ever glad I came home this Christmas!

WALTER: What are you doing home, Stacy? I thought you were, how would you say, pulling yourself together.

STACY: I've done that, thank you. I just came home to look in on the folks, and now I'll be leaving. As soon as I find a coat. (*She looks for her boxes*) Nothing ever changes around here. It's just always exactly the same.

WALTER: That's not entirely true. Some things have changed.

STACY: Like what?

WALTER: Well, Gordon's wife left him, for instance.

GORDON: Shhhh!

WALTER: She took off. Up north. With a bush pilot. Now he thinks people are talking about him.

STACY: Is this true, Gordon?

GORDON: I don't always hear every word they say....

STACY: I mean is it true that what's-her-name....

GORDON: *Carlene.*

STACY: Carlene. She left you?

GORDON: Yep.

STACY: For a bush pilot.

GORDON: Yep.

STACY: So you came back here. To live in this basement.

GORDON: Yeah.

STACY: Pathetic.

She continues looking.

GORDON: Walter's wife is working. On Christmas Eve.

STACY: Typical. Ah ha!

She finds her box and takes out the orange shaggy parka. She tries it on. It is too small, and of an unusual cut.

STACY: Well? What do you think?

GORDON: Uhhhh....

WALTER: I don't think I'd go out wearing that coat, if I were you.

STACY: No?

WALTER: No.

GORDON: (*Overlapping*) No.

Slight pause.

STACY: Does either of you have a cigarette?

WALTER: No.

GORDON: Sorry.

STACY: Damn. I'm going to swoon or something....

WALTER: Help her.

GORDON: You help her.

They help her onto the couch.

GORDON: You want an eggnog?

STACY: You have eggnog?

GORDON: Yeah. I've got eggnog.

STACY: Sure. Give me an eggnog.

He finds a cup, pours her an eggnog, and freshens up his and WALTER's *glasses.*

GORDON: Our supplies are running a bit low.

STACY: What the hell is this?

GORDON: Eggnog.

WALTER: (*Overlapping*) Eggnog.

STACY: What's wrong with it?

WALTER: No milk.

STACY: So what's left?

WALTER: Just the rum and the eggs

GORDON: And nutmeg.

STACY: I can't believe *you're* drinking this, Walter.

WALTER: Actually, it's not bad once you get onto it.

STACY: Really?

WALTER: Takes the edge off. Go ahead. Try it.

STACY: I guess if you're drinking it....

WALTER: Trust me.

ALL: To, uh, hmmmmm....

They drink. Stacy spits hers out.

GORDON: Didn't like it, eh?

STACY: It's disgusting!

WALTER: She's right, you know.

STACY: I can't believe you guys are drinking this!

GORDON: I don't mind it.

STACY: It's horrible.

GORDON: Then don't drink it.

STACY: Why don't you just drink the rum?

GORDON: Straight?!

STACY: Yeah.

WALTER: That makes sense.

GORDON: No way! It's Christmas. We'll drink eggnog, or we won't drink at all.

STACY: Brother! I thought once I got back I'd be OK. Dad just threatened me with the Rotation, Mom worked me over 'cause of my hair, and now there's you guys with your guns trying to poison each other with eggnog. Merry Christmas.

WALTER: Tell me about it.

GORDON: I didn't even try this year. I just came right down here. Just shut the door on the whole thing.

STACY: You didn't even say hi?

GORDON: Nope.

STACY: No wonder Mom's so upset.

GORDON: What?

STACY: You were always her favourite. Our little track star.

GORDON: I hope by now everyone knows I'll never live up to my potential. It's a terrible thing, potential. I wish I'd never shown any.

STACY: You're still the bright light in this family, whether you like it or not.

GORDON: Don't say that! I am not.

STACY: It's true. Right Walter?

WALTER: Absolutely. Which just shows you what a terrible state this family is in.

STACY: No wonder Mom can't get out of bed.

GORDON: It's not my fault.

STACY: Well, whose fault is it then?

WALTER: Don't bicker, you two.

Pause. STACY *looks around.*

STACY: Well, I guess I'll stay down here, at least until I get a coat.

GORDON: I don't think that's going to be possible.

STACY: Why's that?

GORDON: This is my space. Everything you see here, except for the barbed wire, and the boxes, is mine. I converted this old hole into a comfortable living space, and I don't see why you two think you can just breeze in here and take it over.

WALTER: Actually, we just went through some serious negotiations, and basically Gordon and I are going to share the hide-a-bed....

STACY: Ppppptttt! I don't care about your negotiations. This is as much my house as it is yours.

GORDON: This is all your fault, Walter.

WALTER: My fault?

GORDON: Things were going good until you came down. Now look!

STACY: If you don't like it, Gordon, why don't you just leave?

GORDON: I'm not leaving!

STACY: Why not?

GORDON: I was here first!

STACY: So?

GORDON: I got first dibs.

STACY: So?

GORDON: I'm not going anywhere, Stacy. You can't make me.

STACY: Sit down and shut up. It's not my idea of a good Christmas listening to you whine all the time.

GORDON: Who's whining?

STACY: You are.

GORDON: I am not.

STACY: You are too!

GORDON: Am not!

WALTER: Stop sniping at each other! We've got to think about this for a minute.

Pause as they all think.

STACY: We need a plan.

GORDON: You can say that again.

STACY: I'm kind of used to having my days planned out for me. I feel kind of naked without a plan, you know. Kind of vulnerable ...lost.

GORDON: I know that feeling. Kind of trapped at the same time. Like a caged animal.

STACY: No, not trapped, exactly. But lost.

GORDON: Lost, but not trapped.

STACY: Definitely not trapped. But lost. And naked.

GORDON: Naked.

STACY: Buck naked.

GORDON: I don't know. I feel trapped. And lost. But I don't feel naked.

STACY: Well, I feel lost and naked, but not trapped.

WALTER: Shut up! Gosh! I don't want to hear another word out of either of you until you have something constructive to say. I mean it. Not another word. Please.

GORDON: OK.

STACY: Not another word.

GORDON: Shhhhh....

STACY: You shhhh....

Lights fade on basement.

SCENE FIFTEEN

Lights come up on living room. Dad is on his knees, listening in on the

basement conversation by holding his ear to a water glass set on the floor.
He has set a little pedestal table in the middle of the floor. On the table is a
dishpan full of water. The frozen chicken is sitting on DAD'*s chair.*

DAD: I don't know, I don't know, I just don't know. This is not what I
had in mind, when I saw the elk. Not what I had in mind at all.
It's a lot to ask of Walter ... to bring the herd together again. He is
just an adjuster, after all. What does he know about the primal
instincts? Still, he is my number one son ... the fruit of my loins.

He gets up, crosses to his chair, and picks up the chicken, which he sets in
the dishpan with ritualistic intensity. The water spills over the sides of the
pan, so that this action seems like some sort of strange baptism.

There you go, chicken: Thaw. Thaw! How long will it take you
to thaw, I wonder? Do we have enough time? Or is it already too
late? Come on, you stupid bird. Thaw, damn you! (*He pokes at it*)
This is going to take forever....I've never been the kind to stand
idly by waiting for nature to take its course. The only thing that
makes nature at all tolerable is the order we impose on it. I don't
know. I can't see what harm would come of throwing it in the
oven as you are.

Lights fade on DAD *and the chicken.*

But there's a lot riding on you, so we'd better not take any
chances.

Blackout.

SCENE SIXTEEN

Lights come up very slowly on the basement area. In fact, the first six lines
can come out of the darkness.

GORDON: You know what I feel like?

STACY: What?

GORDON: A turkey. A big Butterball turkey with one of those little red
thermometers sticking out of it ...stuffed with raisin bread and
apples and walnuts. A little poultry seasoning and pepper. Broiled
at the last minute to get the skin all nice and crisp and golden
brown.

Pause.

STACY: Or a ham.

GORDON: Ham?

WALTER: Ham?

STACY: Yeah. A big juicy sweltering ham with cloves stuck all over it.

WALTER: Ham?

GORDON: For Christmas?

STACY: Yeah.

WALTER: I've never heard of that.

GORDON: No way. It's turkey or it's not Christmas.

WALTER: Ham for Christmas!

STACY: We always have a choice between turkey and ham. I don't see what the big deal is.

GORDON: The big deal is that ham is not a traditional Christmas meal.

WALTER: The problem you run into is in the potatoes.

STACY: The potatoes?

WALTER: The turkey cries out for mashed potatoes. Mashed with just a bit of milk to make them soft. Whereas the ham begs for scalloped potatoes. Nice and crisp on top, just a-steaming when you put in the spoon. The problem is in cross-potatoing the two. Ham with mashed doesn't cut the mustard, nor does turkey with scallops.

GORDON: That's true. So how do they get around the potato problem out there, Stacy?

STACY: Ham or turkey, turkey or ham. Doesn't matter. They give you the instant mashed ... and the vegetable medley....

WALTER: You know....

GORDON: What?

WALTER: Well, Kenny has that freezer at the back of the store....

STACY: Yeah?

WALTER: It's not impossible to think that he might have a turkey in there, is it?

GORDON: Walter, it's a confectionary.

WALTER: I know.

GORDON: You don't buy turkeys at a confectionary.

WALTER: Wait a minute, just think for a second. Visualize Kenny's, visualize the freezer at the back of Kenny's. What do you see?

GORDON: I see Kenny looking at me in the little round mirror in the corner.

WALTER: You're not even trying.

STACY: I see the cardboard across the top....

WALTER: Good. You see, Gordon?

GORDON: See what?

WALTER: Stacy's visualizing the freezer. What else do you see?

STACY: I see the ice along the side....

WALTER: Good, good. You see, Gordon, your problem is that you have no vision, no imagination. OK, Stacy. Slide the cardboard off the top of the freezer.... Are you sliding the cardboard?

STACY: I'm sliding the cardboard off the top of the freezer.

WALTER: And what do you see?

STACY: There's steam coming up.

WALTER: Good. What is in the freezer?

STACY: I can't make it out.

WALTER: Try Stacy, try.

STACY: There's too much steam.

WALTER: Keep trying, you're almost there.

STACY: I – wait – yes.

WALTER: Yes?

STACY: Yes. I see something. It's yellow, and round, and it's frozen solid.

WALTER: You see! You see, Gordon?!

GORDON: I don't see anything.

WALTER: There's a turkey at Kenny's! I'm sure of it.

GORDON: You're mad!

WALTER: Stacy's seen it!

GORDON: She didn't see anything.

WALTER: All we have to do is go over there, pick it up, throw it in the oven and we have a Christmas dinner.

GORDON: If Kenny's got a turkey in that freezer of his, it's probably ten years old.

WALTER: I'll go check.

STACY: You're going out there?

WALTER: Yes.

GORDON: You're going to Kenny's?

WALTER: Yes. I'm going to Kenny's. I may not have done many worthwhile things in my life before, but tonight I am going to Kenny's to buy a turkey.

GORDON: You got money?

WALTER: I may not have much, but I do have money! And I have a coat. You two take care of each other while I'm gone, will you?

GORDON: We will.

STACY: Good luck out there, Walter.

GORDON: Yeah. Good luck.

WALTER: Thank you. If you don't hear from me in an hour, send help.

WALTER *tentatively, slowly mounts the stairs.*

GORDON: He's a crazy son of a bitch, going out there like that.

STACY: That's what happens when you're the oldest....

Fade to blackout.

Scene Seventeen

DAD *enters* MOTHER*'s room holding the chicken in the dish pan. He sets it on the bed and they stare at it a moment, almost afraid of what it represents.*

MOTHER: You found it.

DAD: Yes. I've set it in water.

MOTHER: Cold water, I hope.

DAD: Well, cool. Lukewarm.

MOTHER: But not hot.

DAD: Definitely not hot.

MOTHER: That's good.

Pause.

DAD: I was monitoring the chicken out in the living room. I felt that by investing a certain amount of psychic energy in the chicken I could speed up the thawing process. I found myself wishing that it was tomorrow morning, that the chicken was cooking away, the children were still here, and Christmas was actually happening in this house again. Is that terribly strange?

MOTHER: No, Darwin. It's not strange at all. It's very much the same as I've been thinking. But then I get frightened. I think I'm hoping for too much. I think if it doesn't work out I'll sink back down, even lower. And you're right, it's not fair to ask you to pick up all the pieces.

DAD: Well, you can't stop hoping.

MOTHER: I don't think I ever did.

Pause.

DAD: So, are you up to cooking this thing tomorrow?

MOTHER: I think so.

DAD: Even if they don't stay? Or won't come up?

MOTHER: You and I could still use some Christmas....

DAD: That's the spirit.

Pause.

DAD: I can't take this, sitting around, waiting for this thing to unfreeze itself. Are you sure there's nothing we can do?

MOTHER: Just like a child waiting for Santa. (*Handing him a hair dryer*) A little something to keep you going.

DAD: You're absolutely brilliant!

MOTHER: Do you really think so?

DAD: Oh yes. Right up there with Lucien Smith and the invention of barbed wire.

MOTHER: You're not putting me in the same league as Lucien Smith.

DAD: No. You're in a league of your own, my dear.

He kisses her, gets up with the hair blower and the chicken. Lights fade as DAD *returns to the living room.*

SCENE EIGHTEEN

Lights up on GORDON *and* STACY *in the basement.* STACY *is rummaging around amid the cardboard boxes.*

GORDON: Careful with those samples. I've already been accused of agitating them.

STACY: I'm not touching his samples.

GORDON: I don't know why he keeps all this old stuff. Unless he's still hoping that Walter or I will follow in his footsteps and go into barbed wire. We were probably the only kids in the world who got Lucien Smith and the history of barbed wire thrown in with the facts of life.

STACY: It gives me the creeps. *(Taking down a box)* What's this. My 5 to 10 box. How come it's open?

GORDON *walks over to one of the boxes, obviously hiding it from* STACY.

GORDON: Although, it's really quite versatile stuff, when you think about it.

STACY: My Barbies should be in here. Gordon?

GORDON: What?

STACY: Why is my 5 to 10 box open?

GORDON: I don't know.

STACY: What happened to my Barbies?

GORDON: How would I know what happened to your Barbies?

STACY: Gordon?

GORDON: What?

STACY: Let me see!

GORDON: I'm not hiding nothing!

She discovers her mutilated Barbie dolls.

STACY: My Barbies! What have you been doing to them?!

GORDON: Nothing!

STACY: How did this get here?

GORDON: What?

STACY: She has a BB in her eye! You were using my Barbies for target practice. Weren't you?!

GORDON: Maybe. Just a bit.

STACY: What kind of pervert would use Barbie dolls for target practice?

GORDON: Well, you used to cut their hair. And stick needles in them. And rip their heads off.

STACY: That's different.

GORDON: What's so different about it?

STACY: I can do whatever I want to Barbie because I'm a girl!

GORDON: What's that got to do with it?

STACY: Barbie's dreams were my dreams. Barbie's life was supposed to be my life. The cars. The clothes. The hair: Right! The bod. And of course, good old Ken. The whole shebang. By nine years old I could tell it wasn't going to work out for me, my God, could I tell! So if I want to shove a burning cigarette into Barbie's face, or stick a needle into her eye, that's my affair. But you have no right to use her for target practice, because you're a boy!

GORDON: I was just bored. I didn't mean anything by it. I'm sorry.

STACY: It doesn't matter anyway. None of this stuff really matters. It's just old stuff. Nothing fits. Just a bunch of old stuff from my useless past that isn't going to do me any good.

STACY *goes back to the cardboard boxes.*

GORDON: You've had an OK kind of, you know, your past....

STACY: Right.

GORDON: You excelled at Brownies. Got all those badges. And I was always pretty amazed at your baton twirling.

STACY: Oh, come on!

GORDON: No. I mean it. Especially when you lit the ends on fire. That was very effective.

STACY: Save it, Gordon. It doesn't matter anyway.

GORDON: No, really. I'm serious.

STACY: Well, thanks.

GORDON: You're welcome.

STACY: There's something I have to say to you, Gordon. If I can get on with my life, there's no reason you can't get on with yours.

GORDON: I am getting on with my life.

STACY: Holed up down this godforsaken basement?

GORDON: It's a start.

STACY: Brother. I don't know. Maybe it's not so bad for you, being down here. You belong in this house – Mom always made sure of that. I've never been anything but a stranger in this house. But at least you had a life going with what's her name Carla. Your own place. A return address. If you had it going once, there's no reason you can't do it again.

GORDON *turns his back on her.*

Why should I start feeling sorry for you? I've got enough to worry about.

She goes back to the boxes.

GORDON: It's *Carlene* ...

She pulls out a box and opens it.

STACY: *Aha!* The tree. The old tree. I knew he wouldn't throw it away.

She pulls out the branches and the centre pole from the box. She gets the centre pole together, set up in the stands and starts putting the branches in it, essentially in random order.

GORDON: What are you doing?

STACY: I'm going to put it together. You want to help?

GORDON: I don't know.

STACY: Come on. Put in a couple of branches.

GORDON: I don't really want to.

STACY: Come on, Gord. Snap out of it. It's Christmas.

GORDON: OK.

He tentatively takes a branch and inserts it into the trunk.

GORDON: Isn't there supposed to be a colour scheme or something?

STACY: Paint seems to have worn off.

GORDON: So how can you tell where they're supposed to go?

STACY: You can't.

They each take some branches and place them in the trunk.

STACY: It's more natural this way.

Fade on STACY *and* GORDON *in a tableau of putting the old tree together as side two of the soundtrack from* My Fair Lady *comes on.*

SCENE NINETEEN

Lights up on living room. DAD *has just put on side two of the soundtrack from* My Fair Lady. *He is thawing the chicken with the hair dryer.*

WALTER *enters, carrying two plastic grocery bags.*

WALTER: Ho Ho Ho!

DAD: *Aiiiigh!*

WALTER: Sorry, Dad. Did I give you a start?

DAD: Where on earth did you come from?

WALTER: I've been out to Kenny's. What are you doing with the hair dryer?

DAD: (*Concealing the chicken*) Oh, just monitoring the effect of forced, heated air on various substances. Too early to share my findings.

WALTER: Listen Dad. I picked up something for you at Kenny's. Here you go. Merry Christmas.

He hands DAD *a small brown paper bag.*

DAD: What's this?

WALTER: It's your Christmas present. Sorry about the wrapping. Open it. Go on.

DAD: You shouldn't have, Walter. (*Opening up the bag*) Fuses!

WALTER: Do you like them?

DAD: Well, isn't that something? You can't have too many fuses...

WALTER: (*Overlapping*) You can't have too many fuses....

DAD: ... that's what I've always said.

WALTER: I hope they're the right size.

DAD: No, they're perfect. I mean, look: there's 15s and 20s in here. They're absolutely perfect. Thank you, Walter.

WALTER: You're welcome, Dad.

DAD: That's very thoughtful. Very thoughtful....

Pause.

WALTER: Well, I guess I should get back downstairs. I got some supplies....

DAD: Sure.

WALTER *crosses the living room, is about to go down the basement, but* DAD *stops him.*

DAD: Walter!

WALTER: Yeah?

DAD: I have a bit of a confession to make to you, Walter. You brought it up earlier and I've been ruminating on it.

WALTER: OK.

DAD: I know you all find it quite convenient to laugh at me, to mock my little quirks, which I know have provided you all with great mirth and amusement over the years. But I was once a young man myself, filled with great dreams, lofty ambitions, courage, hope and – who can remember? Certainly, I was filled with fear, self-doubt, confusion and despair. Who can forget?

The one thing that provided some order and meaning to an otherwise confused existence was Marlin Perkins and "Mutual of Omaha's Wild Kingdom." I know, I know. He had a cartoon woodpecker as a cohost. But at the time, Woody added a certain charm, I thought, anyway.

One evening – one fateful evening – I saw the documentary you referred to earlier. I know that you're right, Walter. The whole thing was a sham. Perkins was a fraud. I know that.

He was my hero! He gave me something to hold on to, something real. He helped shape my reality and my sense of what was ... natural. But when I saw big dumb Jim with a snake on the end of a fishing line, casting it at the brown bear, my heart just broke.

I haven't found anything to replace it. Nothing has come into my life that I can identify with, and that I can use to help define myself.

WALTER: I'm sorry, Dad. I really am.

DAD: Do you know what that feels like? To have everything you've ever believed in undermined?

WALTER: This evening, before I came here, Taffy told me she wanted to talk.

DAD: On Christmas Eve?

WALTER: Yes.

DAD: No one talks ... on Christmas Eve.

WALTER: Exactly. She's not all that happy, and I don't know if I am either. I don't know what would happen if we split, if I'd feel better, or worse. I guess we have a decision to make. When I came here tonight, I was pretty sure I'd left Taffy for good. But now that I've seen (*Discovering the chicken*) how pathetic Gordon is, I'm not so sure.

DAD: Gordon?

WALTER: Gordon's wife left him.

DAD: Well, isn't that something?

WALTER: Dad?

DAD: Yes, son?

WALTER: (*Taking another small paper bag from the plastic bag*) Could you possibly give this to Mom?

DAD: Why, sure. Don't you think you should....

WALTER: I should probably get back downstairs. You know what those two are like.

DAD: Right. Well, I'll take this to your mother then.

WALTER: Thanks.

DAD *leaves.* WALTER *sneaks around his chair, grabs the chicken, puts it into one of his Kenny's bags, and goes downstairs. Blackout.*

Scene Twenty

The stage is in total darkness, then a string of red and green Christmas lights, strung along a length of barbed wire, comes on. From the glow of the lights, the randomly assembled tree can be seen, with GORDON *and* STACY *sitting by it.* WALTER *stands at the top of the stairs.*

WALTER: *Ho Ho Ho!*

STACY: Santa!

He comes down stairs and joins STACY *and* GORDON.

STACY: What do you think of the tree?

WALTER: It's the most beautiful tree I've ever seen.

GORDON: We call it a random pine.

STACY: The colour coding has worn off the branches.

WALTER: Yes, I heard.

STACY: Do you like the lights? We strung them on some Gliddons coil cactus point variation.

WALTER: It looks beautiful ... like a magazine or something.

GORDON: You got to Kenny's?

WALTER: Oh yeah ... I got there all right ... You'll never believe this: He remembered me!

GORDON: Are you serious?

WALTER: He was there, behind the counter. Same grey cardigan, still working the pick back and forth. He looks up and he says, "Hello, Walter." Haven't seen the guy in twenty years and he says hello to me like I was just in there yesterday ... I never even knew he knew my name.

GORDON: I don't believe it.

WALTER: Wait. There's more. He shook my hand.

GORDON: Kenny touched you?

WALTER: Oh yes. We had a real moment ... I told him that the security light on top of his pole reminded me of the star of the east ... I don't think he knew what I was talking about. And look!

STACY: What did you get, what did you get?

WALTER: Behold, ye of little faith.

He pulls out the chicken.

STACY: A turkey!

WALTER: It's actually a chicken, but close enough.

GORDON: I don't believe it!

WALTER: It's the magic of Christmas, Gordon.

GORDON *takes and cradles the chicken in his arms.*

GORDON: It's the most beautiful chicken I've ever seen.

Slight pause as they watch GORDON *fondle the chicken.*

WALTER: I managed to get a few other things, too. Stacy. Come here and sit on Santa's knee. That's a girl. Don't be afraid.

STACY: (*Sitting on his knee*) I'm not afraid.

WALTER: Have you been a good girl?

STACY: Oh yes, Santa. I've been very good.

WALTER: You're sure about that?

STACY: Honest. Cross my heart and hope to die ... stick a needle in my eye.

WALTER: OK. Let's see what Santa has here for the good little girl.

He gives her a package of cigarettes.

STACY: Oh, thank you Santa. God, thank you, thank you.

WALTER: And here's a lighter to help you get those things going.

STACY: Thank you Santa. This is wonderful.

WALTER: Give Santa a kiss. (*She does.*)

STACY: Oh boy, I've been dreaming of this.

She opens the pack, takes out a cigarette and lights up. They watch her smoke.

WALTER: Hello, little boy.

GORDON: Hi, Santa.

WALTER: What's your name?

GORDON: Gordon.

WALTER: Have you been a good little boy, Gordon?

GORDON: Yes, Santa.

WALTER: OK. Let's see what Santa has for you. Let's see ... here are some eggs ... and some milk.

GORDON: That's it? Eggs and milk?

WALTER: What's wrong with that?

GORDON: Kind of functional presents, don't you think?

WALTER: Maybe we have something else in here....

GORDON, *still clutching the chicken to his breast, comes over and sits on* WALTER's *knee.*

Let's see ... oh yes. Look what else Santa found at Kenny's. (*Pulls out a package of BBs.*)

GORDON: BBs! Oh wow! Kenny had BBs?

WALTER: He's got everything.

GORDON: Oh, thank you, Santa, thank you.

WALTER: You're welcome, little boy. Just don't go shooting your brother or your sister with them. Now, do you know what you could do for Santa?

GORDON: What?

WALTER: Make some more eggnog.

GORDON: Yeah. With milk and everything....

GORDON *goes about mixing the rum, eggs and milk in the punch bowl.*

STACY: (*So* GORDON *can't hear*) So, where'd you get the chicken?

WALTER: Kenny's.

STACY: Right. Like Kenny has chickens all of the sudden. Where'd you get it?

WALTER: Upstairs.

STACY: You stole it?

WALTER: Yes. Dad had it in the living room. He was thawing it with a hair dryer.

STACY: You think they've been planning a Christmas dinner?

WALTER: It looks that way.

STACY: I'm not going up there to eat with them. No way.

WALTER: It's warm up there.

STACY: The Rotation is up there. Mom's hair concerns are up there. It just won't work out.

GORDON: What are you guys talking about?

STACY: Walter wants to go upstairs.

GORDON: What for?

STACY: So we can eat the chicken.

GORDON: No way.

WALTER: What do you mean no way?

GORDON: You're not touching my chicken. She's mine. No one's eating her.

STACY: Brother!

WALTER: How about some eggnog? Is the eggnog ready, Gordon?

They fill their glasses. GORDON *is careful to keep his distance. Quick toast and they drink.*

WALTER: You guys wouldn't have any way of knowing this because you don't work. But where I work they hold these seminars from time to time and what they do is bring in these facilitators who have a flip chart and different coloured markers and they put your ideas up on these flip charts and at the end of the day you can see what it is you've been talking about.

GORDON: That's dumb.

WALTER: But it works. Anyway, what I'm proposing is this. We throw up our situation on a flip chart and then maybe we'll be able to develop some sort of action plan to guide us over the next couple of hours.

GORDON: We don't have a flip chart.

STACY: Or markers.

WALTER: That's OK. We'll use our imaginations and visualize.

WALTER *mimes the flipchart and markers.*

So here's the flipchart. I'm going to draw a line down the middle of the flipchart. Like so.

GORDON: What colour is that?

WALTER: It's black.

GORDON: Why black?

WALTER: Because black is neutral.

STACY: Like hell it is.

WALTER: OK. What colour would you like the line to be?

GORDON: Blue.

STACY: I can live with that.

WALTER: OK. Blue it is.

GORDON: Uh uh uh. You've got to tear that sheet off and start again.

WALTER: OK. *(He tears the sheet off)* Here we go. A blue line. Now, up at the top here, I'm going to write: *Upstairs – colon – eat the chicken.* In green. OK? Good. And on the other side of the line up top here, I'm going to write: *Downstairs – colon – don't eat the chicken.* In red. OK? Good. Now. I want you two to give me points for either side, and I'll write them in. Stacy? Give me one good reason why we should go upstairs and eat the chicken.

STACY: OK.

Pause.

WALTER: Stacy?

STACY: Don't rush me! Hunger.

WALTER: Very good, Stacy. I'll just write that in under *Eat the chicken:* Hunger. We're all hungry and that's a good reason for going upstairs to eat the chicken. Gordon?

GORDON: What?

WALTER: Now you give me one good reason why we shouldn't eat the chicken. And stay down here.

GORDON: OK.

Pause.

WALTER: We're waiting.

GORDON: OK. I am fond of the chicken.

WALTER: You're fond of the chicken. Is that what you want me to write?

GORDON: Yes.

WALTER: *(Writing)* Gordon fond of chicken ... there we go. Good. Now. Anything else we could add to our list? Either side?

STACY: The environment?

WALTER: The environment?

STACY: Yes.

WALTER: Is that a red one or a green one?

STACY: I'm not sure.

WALTER: Maybe we'll just leave that one. Gordon?

GORDON: What?

WALTER: Any other thoughts you'd like to share with us?

GORDON: No.

WALTER: OK. Good. You guys are great. Now I'd like to move from the realm of action into the consequences of our actions. On the green side, in the *Go upstairs and eat the chicken* category, there are some obvious outcomes. Like satisfying our hunger. Getting warm. Salvaging some kind of Christmas from the dung heap of dysfunction. Now, on the red side, we have *Stay down here and don't eat the chicken.* What are the consequences?

WALTER *stares out at the flip chart but ends up delivering this directly to* GORDON.

Eventually the chicken thaws. But Gordon has no way of preserving or cooking the chicken, and watches in horror as his beloved bird begins to rot and decompose before his very eyes. We know what keeps down here and what doesn't. Don't we, Gordon? We know that in a matter of only a few hours that chicken will have to be eaten, or its flesh will start to putrefy. Christmas will be over. Stacy and I will be gone. It will just be you down here ... lurching around in an eggnog-induced stupor, clutching your rancid chicken to your breast. *Is that what you want?!*

GORDON: Yes. No. I don't know!

WALTER: C'mon, Gordon.

GORDON: No!

WALTER: *We're going upstairs, Gordon!*

GORDON: Stacy?

STACY: What can I tell you, Gordy? When you see it all up on the flip chart like that, it seems like we should go up and eat the chicken.

GORDON: OK.

WALTER: That's a good boy.

STACY: What do we do now?

WALTER: We take the tree, and the lights, and the eggnog, and the chicken – and we go upstairs and have a good old-fashioned Christmas with Mom and Dad.

GORDON: He won't let us up with this tree. He'll think it's an abomination. He doesn't want Christmas.

WALTER: Then we'll force the issue. You've got BBs now.

STACY: That's right. You're armed!

GORDON: What about Mom?

STACY: The Condition.

WALTER: Say hello to her, Gordon. That's all she wanted in the first place.

GORDON: Really?

WALTER: Just think, the smell of this chicken wafting through the house. It'll be just like Christmas. Come on. Are we going to do this or not?

GORDON: I guess.

WALTER: Stacy?

STACY: All right.

WALTER: OK.

GORDON: I'll take the chicken, if you don't mind.

WALTER: OK. You take the chicken. I'll get the tree and the lights. Stacy, bring the eggnog. Ready?!

STACY: Ready.

GORDON: I'll go first and scout it out.

WALTER: OK. Let's go!

WALTER *pulls the plug and grabs the wire,* STACY *grabs the punch bowl,* GORDON *leads the assault on the living room. In very faint light, we see their assault on the main floor throughout the next scene.*

SCENE TWENTY-ONE

MOTHER's *room. Flashlight clicks on. There is no eyeball. The flashlight swings around wildly.* MOTHER *laughs, then clicks on a light.*

DAD: You're up!

MOTHER: Yes, I'm up.

DAD: How do you feel?

MOTHER: Good. Better than before.

DAD: That's good.

MOTHER: Good enough to get the stuffing made for the bird. I think I'll add some raisins. Gordon always likes my stuffing when I add raisins. Has it thawed?

DAD: It's well on its way.

MOTHER: Isn't it funny, when the Hutterites came by that day I just had a notion that we might be needing a chicken.

Slight pause.

DAD: Walter brought me a Christmas present from Kenny's.

MOTHER: What did he bring?

DAD: Fuses!

MOTHER: Ordinary household fuses?

DAD: Yes.

DAD: Yes. I was so touched....

MOTHER: Fuses.

DAD: And he asked me to give you this.

Hands her a paper bag.

MOTHER: Well, isn't that nice. A night light. How thoughtful. We haven't had one of these in this house for a while.

Slight pause.

DAD: Walter also told me some interesting news from the basement. Gordon's wife left him.

MOTHER: Maybe now he can get on with his life.

Pause.

MOTHER: I think there's only one thing to do, Darwin.

DAD: What's that?

MOTHER: Go down and get Gordon – and Stacy and Walter. And invite them all up for dinner.

DAD: Are you up to it?

MOTHER: I think I am. Are you?

DAD: I suppose I'm prepared to kick at the turf and sniff the air, protect the herd.

MOTHER: Does that mean yes?

DAD: Yes.

MOTHER: Shall we, then?

They leave the bedroom, turning out the light as they leave.

SCENE TWENTY-TWO

As the bedroom light is turned off, the strand of barbed wire lights comes on, revealing GORDON, *clutching the gun and the chicken,* STACY *and* WALTER *in the living room. The barbed wire has been wrapped around the tree, making it seem that the tree is in some kind of cage.*

MOTHER *and* DAD *enter.*

MOTHER: Look, Darwin. A family Christmas. How touching.

DAD: The tree! My wire!

MOTHER: Gordon? What are you doing with that chicken?

GORDON: I'm holding it.

MOTHER: Why are you doing that?

GORDON: Because it's mine.

MOTHER: Give it to me.

GORDON: I don't think so.

MOTHER: I said give it to me.

GORDON: But Mom....

MOTHER: Bring it here.

He gives her the chicken.

That's a good boy. We have to cook this chicken. And eat it. But you can help me with the stuffing. OK?

GORDON: OK.

MOTHER: That's my boy. Now give me a hug.

He does.

MOTHER: What's the big idea, not coming in to see me?

GORDON: I don't know, Mom. I was embarrassed, I guess.

MOTHER: Because of Carla?

GORDON: *Carlene.*

MOTHER: None of us really liked her.

GORDON: Really?

MOTHER: We just pretended to like her, for your sake.

GORDON: That was nice of you.

MOTHER: And now that she's gone, you can start living up to your potential.

GORDON: Ah, Mom....

MOTHER: Walter. I want to thank you for the present. That was very thoughtful.

WALTER: You're welcome.

MOTHER: Better to light one little candle than to curse the darkness. And Stacy. What can I say? I'm sorry. We'll do something with your hair in the morning.

STACY: Oh yeah....

STACY *and* MOTHER *sit on the couch. The men mill around. No one seems to know what to do next.*

MOTHER: My, doesn't the old tree look nice, Darwin?

DAD: The tree looks good.

STACY: Gordon called it random pine because we didn't know where to put the branches.

DAD: Many a night I struggled with that blasted tree.

MOTHER: And don't the lights look nice, Darwin?

DAD: They do look nice. Is that Gliddons coil cactus point variation?

STACY: Sure is.

DAD: Ah, to see the wire against the old pine tree like that. Brings back my youth. Yep. Sure does.

MOTHER: Don't start in on your youth now, dear.

Pause.

STACY: Now what'll we do?

GORDON: Who says we have to do anything?

STACY: What would a normal family do in this situation?

GORDON: Watch TV?

MOTHER: We're not watching TV tonight, Gordon.

GORDON: Just an idea.

DAD: We could listen to the next record in the Rotation.

STACY: Oh, brother.

MOTHER: What is the next record, Darwin?

DAD: Album #194: *Real German Oom-Pah Songs From the Hofbrau House in Munich.*

STACY: Great.

MOTHER: I don't think we want to hear the "Beer Barrel Polka" right now.

STACY: You can say that again.

WALTER: We could always sing a carol.

STACY: Sing a carol?

WALTER: Yeah.

STACY: I don't know if I'm up to that.

DAD: I haven't sung in years.

GORDON: I don't want to sing a carol. It brings back bad memories of Grade One. Mrs. Patterson took me aside and told me just to mouth the words.

MOTHER: She didn't!

GORDON: She sure did. I haven't sung since.

STACY: I don't think I know the words to any carols.

WALTER: What about the Christmas tree one? You know: "O Christmas Tree, O Christmas Tree."

STACY: I don't think I know it.

GORDON: I can't sing that.

WALTER: Sure you can.

MOTHER: I think singing a carol is a wonderful idea, Walter. But maybe we need some time, to knit as a group, before singing.

WALTER: Let's just gather 'round and try it, OK?!

No one gathers 'round.

WALTER: Come on, you guys.

DAD: You're making us all feel self-conscious.

WALTER: I don't care how you feel. I want to sing a carol like a normal family so let's gather 'round, damn it!

GORDON: How about we just have some eggnog?

WALTER: *(Grabbing the gun)* First we'll gather 'round and sing the goddamned carol, and then we'll drink some more eggnog, Gordon, OK?

GORDON: OK, OK.

WALTER: Now gather 'round, for Christ's sake. All of you.

They gather 'round.

WALTER: That's better. Now we're going to do the Christmas tree one. OK?

ALL: OK.

WALTER: Ready?

ALL: Ready.

WALTER: OK. Here we go.

WALTER *leads the song, still with gun in hand.*

ALL: "O Christmas Tree, O Christmas Tree
"How lovely are thy branches.
"O Christmas Tree, O Christmas Tree
"Ya dee da da, dee da da."

There is an awkward pause as they realize none of them, even WALTER, *has any clear idea of what the words are. They charge energetically into the next bars, nonetheless.*

"Ya da dee da, da da dee dee
"Ya doo dee doo, da doo dee dee
"O Christmas Tree, O Christmas Tree
"How lovely are thy branches."

MOTHER: You can put the gun down now, Walter.

WALTER: Yes, Mom.

MOTHER: I swear to God, someday someone's going to lose an eye because of that stupid thing.

Unnoticed by the others, DAD *slips out of the living room.*

GORDON: You always have to be the boss, don't you?

WALTER: That's not true.

GORDON: Just 'cause you have a job.

WALTER: What's wrong with having a job?

STACY: You have to lord it over us all the time.

WALTER: I don't lord it over you! I don't even see you. (*To* GORDON) I don't hear you complaining about the fact that I have a job when I'm offering to pay your rent for you.

GORDON: Well then, don't pay my rent! See what I care!

MOTHER: Children, children, children. Stop your fighting.

GORDON: He started it.

STACY: Yeah.

WALTER: I did not.

STACY: You did too.

WALTER: I didn't start anything! It's you two. Always ganging up on me. Ever since we were kids.

GORDON: Right!

STACY: As if!

MOTHER: Darwin, do something about your children, for heaven's sake. Darwin? Where did your father go?

DAD *enters, cradling Handel's* Messiah *in his arms.*

DAD: Here I am. I thought we could use this.

MOTHER: What is it?

DAD: I give you Album # 280: I give you Handel's *Messiah.*

STACY: Christmas music!

GORDON: (*Taking the record*) Wow! Does this have "Frosty the Snowman" on it?

DAD: No it doesn't have "Frosty the Snowman" on it. It's Handel's *Messiah.*

STACY: Daddy – you've broken the Rotation.

DAD: I'm aware of that.

MOTHER: Thank you, Darwin.

DAD: I suppose it had to be done. Gordon....

GORDON: Yeah?

DAD: I'll put it on, if you don't mind. I have a bit of a system.

He puts on his white cotton gloves and changes the record on the turntable.

WALTER: Gordon, could you pour the eggnog?

MOTHER: I could sure use an eggnog.

GORDON *pours out eggnogs for all.*

MOTHER: Come on, Darwin! Play the damned thing.

He puts on the Messiah.

WALTER: Merry Christmas, everyone.

ALL: Merry Christmas.

WALTER: To family! ...

The rest of the family avoids this toast. Handel's Messiah *comes up, sounding old and scratchy despite* DAD's *great care. Slowly the lights on the barbed wire fade to blackout.*

THE END

Eugene Stickland's short fiction has appeared in anthologies such as *Sundogs, Saskatchewan Gold* and *200% Cracked Wheat*. Although Stickland began his university education in music, he completed a MFA degree in Theatre and is now the author of plays such as: *darkness on the edge of town, Quartet,* and *The Family*. Stickland also spent some time teaching at the University of Regina, and writing for film, television and theatre. After recently being named Playwright-in-Residence at ATP, Stickland moved to Calgary where he is working on two new plays and a novel.